TABLE OF CONTENTS

➤━●━◄

CHAPTER   **PAGE #**

1   YOUR ASSIGNMENT IS ANY PROBLEM YOU WERE   3
CREATED TO SOLVE ON EARTH

2   WHAT YOU LOVE IS A CLUE TO THE GIFTS AND   5
WISDOM YOU CONTAIN TO COMPLETE YOUR
ASSIGNMENT

3   WHAT YOU HATE IS A CLUE TO SOMETHING YOU   9
ARE ASSIGNED TO CORRECT

4   WHAT GRIEVES YOU IS A CLUE TO SOMETHING   11
YOU ARE ASSIGNED TO HEAL

5   IF YOU REBEL AGAINST YOUR ASSIGNMENT,   13
GOD MAY PERMIT PAINFUL EXPERIENCES
TO CORRECT YOU

6   YOUR ASSIGNMENT WILL REQUIRE SEASONS   17
OF PREPARATION

7   YOU WILL ONLY SUCCEED WHEN YOUR   23
ASSIGNMENT BECOMES AN OBSESSION

Unless otherwise indicated, all Scripture quotations are taken from the King James Version of the Bible.
7 Signposts to Your Assignment, Seeds of Wisdom on Your Assignment, Topic 22
ISBN 1-56394-117-1/B-122
Copyright © 2007 **MIKE MURDOCK**
All publishing rights belong exclusively to Wisdom International
Publisher/Editor: Deborah Murdock Johnson
Published by The Wisdom Center · 4051 Denton Hwy. · Ft. Worth, TX 76117
1-817-759-0300
You Will Love Our Website...! WisdomOnline.com

Accuracy Department: To our Friends and Partners...We welcome any comments on errors or misprints you find in our book...Email our department: AccuracyDept@thewisdomcenter.tv. Your aid in helping us excel is highly valued.

You Will Only Be Remembered
For Two Things:
The Problems You Solve
Or The Ones You Create.

-MIKE MURDOCK

∽ 1 ∽

Your Assignment Is Any Problem You Were Created To Solve On Earth

Creativity Is The Search For Solutions.
Let me illustrate. In large gatherings of the past, speakers could not be heard clearly. So, microphones and public address systems were created. Eyeglasses were created for those who have difficulty seeing.

Problems are the catalysts for *creativity.* When an inventor—whether it is Thomas Edison or whomever—invents something, his creativity is based on an existing problem. He *solves* the problem, and he is *rewarded* accordingly.

Why did you buy your car? Because it solved a transportation problem. Why do you watch the news each evening on television? It solves an information problem. So, every *part* of you has an *Assignment,* a problem to solve. Your eyes have the Assignment of *seeing.* Your ears solve the problem of *hearing.*

That is why God created us. God wanted a *love* relationship. He wanted to be *chosen, pursued* and *treasured.* So, He created Adam and Eve.

Adam had a problem. So, God created a solution, Eve. "And the Lord God said, It is not good that the man should be alone; I will make him an help meet for him," (Genesis 2:18). Each one of us is a *solution.*

When you open your eyes every morning, you are looking into an entire world *crammed* with *solutions*. Everything created is a solution...to somebody, somewhere, at some time.

You Are A Solution To Somebody.

You are a reward to someone.

Somebody *needs* you.

Somebody *wants* you.

You are *necessary* to somebody, somewhere... *today*.

You were created for a specific and very special purpose...*to solve a specific problem on earth*.

I call this, *The Assignment.* (See Jeremiah 1:4-5.)

God will assist you in *your Assignment.* "For thou shalt go to all that I shall send thee, and whatsoever I command thee thou shalt speak. Be not afraid of their faces: for I am with thee to deliver thee, saith the Lord," (Jeremiah 1:7-8).

It Is Essential That You Discover Your Assignment And Give Yourself Totally To It. "Let every man abide in the same calling wherein he was called," (1 Corinthians 7:20).

Everything was created to bring pleasure to God. "Thou art worthy, O Lord, to receive glory and honour and power: for Thou hast created all things, and for Thy pleasure they are and were created," (Revelation 4:11).

Your Assignment Is To Solve Problems For Those To Whom You Are Sent.

Remember: *Your Assignment Is Any Problem You Were Created To Solve On Earth.*

≈ 2 ≈

What You Love Is A Clue To The Gifts And Wisdom You Contain To Complete Your Assignment

———————➤⊰◦⊱◄———————

Love Is The Map To Your Wisdom.
When you have a love for children, a special Wisdom begins to grow and develop in you for children. You begin to understand their fears, tears and desires. When you have a love for animals, you develop an intuition, a special Wisdom for their behavior and conduct. You can sense what they are feeling. When you need Wisdom in your marriage, love for your mate must be birthed first.
Wisdom Is The Product of Love.
Love Births Persistence. When you love something, you give birth to extraordinary tenacity, determination and persistence. Recently, I read a powerful story about a runner. In his youth, he had a terrible disease. Doctors insisted he would never be able to even walk again. But, something powerful was already within him...his love for running.
His love for running birthed *determination.* He ended up winning a gold medal in the Olympics.
Love is stronger than sickness. It is stronger than disease. It is stronger than poverty.
Find what you truly love, and *build your daily*

agenda around it.

You contain certain qualities, special gifts and worthy traits. They make you *unique.* You are distinct from the herd. What is it? What do you *love to talk* about the *most? Think* about most?

I discussed this with my staff recently. "If every human on earth was paid $10 an hour for work, regardless of the type of job, what would you choose to do? For example, if you chose to be a janitor of a building, you would receive $10 an hour for it. If you decided that you wanted to be a heart surgeon, you would still receive $10 an hour. What would you love to do if money was not involved?" *That Is Your Life Assignment.*

Moses loved people. When he saw an Egyptian beating a fellow Israelite, he moved quickly. In his passion for justice he killed the Egyptian. That was unfortunate. It postponed his Assignment. But his love for his people was a clue to his mantle as a Deliverer. He was attentive to their *cries. He cared.* His compassion ran deep. Because he had a love for people, he was able to lead people.

Abraham loved peace. He despised conflict. So when God decided to destroy Sodom and Gomorrah, Abraham became an intercessor and mediator for Lot, his nephew, who lived in Sodom. His love for peace and justice was rewarded by God. Though Sodom and Gomorrah were destroyed, Lot and his daughters were brought out safely. It happened because Abraham contained something very precious: a love for peace. *His love for peace birthed the Wisdom necessary to achieve it.*

Recently, a close friend of mine came to our ministry and gave a special teaching. He gave us a personality profile that enabled us to discover the greatest gifts within us. He showed us how to examine the lives of Bible characters and how to relate to them. This is one of the most important things you can do. You must find what you really care about and develop your life around it.

It is wise to correct the flaws within you.

It is even wiser to acknowledge and embrace your dominant gifts and expertise.

Permit the *true you* to emerge. I have often heard people insist to a shy person, "You must talk more!" Then the same person will turn to someone talking a lot and say, "Be quiet! Just sit and listen!"

We instruct youth, "Get more serious about life."

We instruct the elderly, "You need to be less serious!"

Do not move away from the essence of what God made you. Understand the importance of your *uniqueness*. Your distinctions must be discovered, embraced and celebrated.

Sameness Creates Comfort.

Difference Creates Reward.

Discern your gifts. *Identify* your difference. Build your daily agenda around it. Whatever you are *gifted* to do is what you should be doing.

Remember: *What You Love Is A Clue To The Gifts And Wisdom You Contain To Complete Your Assignment.*

You Can Only Conquer
Something
You Hate.

-MIKE MURDOCK

WHAT YOU HATE IS A CLUE TO SOMETHING YOU ARE ASSIGNED TO CORRECT

Anger Is Passion.

It simply requires *appropriate focus.* Have you ever wondered why others were not angry about situations that infuriated *you?* Of course you have.

Anger is a clue to your Assignment.

Moses hated slavery. When he saw an Egyptian beating an Israelite, fury arose. Why? He was a Deliverer.

3 Wisdom Keys In Understanding Anger

▶ You Cannot Correct What You Are Unwilling To Confront.

▶ Anything Permitted Will Increase.

▶ What You Can Tolerate You Cannot Change.

I love Wisdom.

I hate ignorance. I have attended seminars where Scriptures were misquoted, truth was distorted, and error was dominant. It was almost impossible to sit and permit it to be spoken without my open confrontation to it.

You cannot really change or correct something unless you have a God-given hatred for it, whether it is sickness, injustice, racial prejudice, poverty, divorce or abortion. My friend, Pastor Mike Hayes, calls it, "a Holy Hatred."

Many things are wrong in this country, but they will never be changed until *someone is angry enough* about it to step forward and take charge.

For instance, abortion has slowly become accepted, although it is a truly devastating blight on the moral landscape of this country. It appears that no true and articulate spokesperson has yet emerged who is capable of turning the tide. I thank God for those who are making significant efforts to do so!

The Persuaded Become The Persuasive.

I have asked God often to raise up someone with a burning desire who can *successfully* plead the case of the unborn child. I have asked God to provide a militant, intellectual, passionate zealot who will link The Word of God with the gift of life in my generation—someone passionate and on fire.

That someone could be you.

I am not justifying the bombing of abortion clinics. That is as hypocritical as the abortionist.

I am speaking of *an anointing*, a mantle, a calling when someone *rises up* to complete their Assignment in this generation: to uproot the Seeds of rebellion growing in us.

Your anger is important. Very important. It simply needs an appropriate focus.

Do not ignore it. Satan dreads your fury.

An angry man is an awakened man. Only an angry man can change the mind of the unconcerned.

Anger alone cures apathy.

Focused Fury Is The Key To Change.

Remember: *What You Hate Is A Clue To Something You Are Assigned To Correct.*

WHAT GRIEVES YOU IS A CLUE TO SOMETHING YOU ARE ASSIGNED TO HEAL

Tears Talk.

Whatever makes you *weep* is a clue to something you were created to heal.

Compassion Is A Signpost.

What grieves you? Battered wives? Abused or molested children? Ignorance? Disease? Poverty? Pornography? Homosexuality? Abortion? Identify it. Be honest with yourself.

Caring qualifies you as an *Instrument of Healing.*

What makes you cry is a clue to a problem God has anointed you to change, conquer and heal. Remember Nehemiah? His heart was broken about the walls of Jerusalem needing repair. He could not sleep. He wept long hours.

He was stirred to write letters, contact officials, and even change his personal life to rebuild the walls.

Examine Ezra. His heart was distressed over the temple in Jerusalem. He could not rest. He wept. He knew what few knew.

The presence of God is the only cure for wounded people. He recognized that places mattered and that God would honor and reward those who sanctified a worship center in the city.

Feelings Are Often Signposts To Your Assignment.

Social insanity is epidemic. Observe how the liquor industry has their signs on every billboard of a stadium. Every newspaper contains liquor advertisements. Yet alcohol has killed more people on our highways than those killed in the entire Vietnam Conflict.

Someone said we have lost more of our children to death by alcoholism than deaths in all the major wars. Yet everyone screams about the horrors of war while sipping their alcohol at a cocktail table.

Your Greatest Enemy Is Always Within You.

Someday, God is going to raise up another Billy Sunday or someone who is sickened at the children's brains splattered on a highway. Someone is going to be so grieved over senseless deaths that their Assignment becomes clear. That Assignment will *become their obsession.* Then, they will rise up to launch a war...a holy war that will salvage the lives of thousands and *heal the broken* in this generation.

Have you wept long hours over financial bankruptcy and debt? Think of the many families in America who lack finances because of a father's drinking habit. Think of the children who cannot be put through school because money is wasted on alcohol. Do you weep when you see homeless children?

Tears Are Clues To Where God Will Use You Most.

Oh, there are many things that should set us on fire. What *grieves* you? What *saddens* you? What *moves you* to tears? Pay attention to it.

Remember: *What Grieves You Is A Clue To Something You Are Assigned To Heal.*

5

If You Rebel Against Your Assignment, God May Permit Painful Experiences To Correct You

God Cannot Be Ignored Without A Consequence.

God can create painful experiences and unforgettable experiences.

Jonah is a perfect example. He rebelled against God's instructions to, "Arise, go to Nineveh, that great city, and cry against it; for their wickedness is come up before Me. But Jonah rose up to flee unto Tarshish from the presence of the Lord, and went down to Joppa; and he found a ship going to Tarshish: so he paid the fare thereof, and went down into it, to go with them unto Tarshish from the presence of the Lord. But the Lord sent out a great wind into the sea, and there was a mighty tempest in the sea, so that the ship was like to be broken," (Jonah 1:2-4).

Jonah had to endure three miserable days and nights in the belly of the fish before he *accepted* his Assignment.

Never Misjudge God.

He never ignores tiny acts of defiance.

Examine the life of Joshua. When Achan rebelled and kept some of the spoils of war, they lost the first battle of Ai. In a single day, their reputation was stained. Joshua's men lost total confidence. Achan had ignored the command of God. Consequently, the entire nation suffered defeat until obedience became their priority again.

The Disobedience of One Can Create Corporate Judgment On Many. When one defies the will of God, everyone involved *must pay the price for it.*

A well-known leader said God spoke to him when finances became difficult for his ministry. "Someone on your staff does not belong." He fired the staff member. The finances flowed again. *When Wrong People Leave Your Life, Wrong Things Stop Happening.*

Pain Is Corrective. It happens often in The Potter's House, where our Father is remolding *common clay vessels for uncommon exploits.* "It is good for me that I have been afflicted; that I might learn Thy statutes," (Psalm 119:71).

The Waves of Yesterday's Disobedience Will Splash On The Shores of Today For A Season. If you are walking in contradiction to God's laws, expect painful experiences on the road ahead.

Do not waste these Hurting Seasons.

That is where the healing process begins.

6 Rewards of Pain

1. Pain forces you to *look*...
   ...to The Word of God for answers.
2. Pain forces you to *lean*...
   ...on the arm of God, instead of men.
3. Pain forces you to *learn*...
   ...where you went astray.
4. Pain forces you to *long*...
   ...for His presence and healing.

5.   Pain forces you to *listen*...
             ...for changes in God's instructions.
6.   Pain forces you to *love*...
             ...whatever remains.

Remember: *If You Rebel Against Your Assignment, God May Permit Painful Experiences To Correct You.*

An Uncommon Future
Will Require
Uncommon Preparation.

-MIKE MURDOCK

YOUR ASSIGNMENT WILL REQUIRE SEASONS OF PREPARATION

You Are Not Born Qualified—You Become Qualified.
Moses required preparation. He spent his first 40 years learning the Wisdom of the Egyptians. "And Moses was learned in all the Wisdom of the Egyptians, and was mighty in words and in deeds. And when he was full forty years old, it came into his heart to visit his brethren the children of Israel," (Acts 7:22-23).

He spent another 40 years learning the lessons of leadership and priesthood. "Now Moses kept the flock of Jethro his father in law, the priest of Midian: and he led the flock to the backside of the desert, and came to the mountain of God, even to Horeb," (Exodus 3:1).

"And when forty years were expired, there appeared to him in the wilderness of mount Sina an angel of the Lord in a flame of fire in a bush. When Moses saw it, he wondered at the sight: and as he drew near to behold it, the voice of the Lord came unto him," (Acts 7:30-31).

Moses was a protégé for 80 years.

His first 40 years educated him about *enemies*.

His second 40 years educated him about *people*.

Preparation. *Preparation.* PREPARATION.

Jesus required preparation. Jesus spent 30 years preparing for His ministry. "And Jesus Himself began to be about thirty years of age," (Luke 3:23). These days seem so different for young ministers. The average young minister wants to prepare for three-and-a-half years for 30 years of public ministry. Jesus did the opposite. *He prepared for 30 years for a public ministry of three-and-a-half years.*

The Apostle Paul required preparation. He was a Pharisee and the son of a Pharisee. (See Acts 23:6.) He had invested years of preparation for the intelligentsia of his generation. "If any other man thinketh that he hath whereof he might trust in the flesh, I more: Circumcised the eighth day, of the stock of Israel, of the tribe of Benjamin, an Hebrew of the Hebrews; as touching the law, a Pharisee; Concerning zeal, persecuting the church; touching the righteousness which is in the law, blameless," (Philippians 3:4-6).

The 11 Seasons of Preparation For Your Assignment

1. Seasons of *Affliction*. "...but be thou partaker of the afflictions of the gospel according to the power of God," (2 Timothy 1:8). "It is good for me that I have been afflicted; that I might learn Thy statutes," (Psalm 119:71).

2. Seasons of *Chastening*. "For whom the Lord loveth He chasteneth, and scourgeth every son whom He receiveth. Now no chastening for the present seemeth to be joyous, but grievous: nevertheless afterward it yieldeth the peaceable fruit of righteousness unto them which are exercised thereby," (Hebrews 12:6, 11).

3. Seasons of *Contention*. "But foolish and unlearned questions avoid, knowing that they do gender strifes. And the servant of the Lord must not strive; but be gentle unto all men, apt to teach, patient," (2 Timothy 2:23-24).

   4.   **Seasons of *Credibility*.** "But watch thou in all things, endure afflictions, do the work of an evangelist, make full proof of thy ministry," (2 Timothy 4:5).

   5.   **Seasons of *Disappointment*.** "For Demas hath forsaken me, having loved this present world, and is departed unto Thessalonica," (2 Timothy 4:10).

   6.   **Seasons of *Injustice*.**   "Alexander the coppersmith did me much evil: the Lord reward him according to his works," (2 Timothy 4:14).

   7.   **Seasons of *Isolation*.** "At my first answer no man stood with me, but all man forsook me: I pray God that it may not be laid to their charge," (2 Timothy 4:16).

   8.   **Seasons of *Persecution*.**   "Persecutions, afflictions, which came unto me...what persecutions I endured: but out of them all the Lord delivered me. Yea, and all that will live godly in Christ Jesus shall suffer persecution," (2 Timothy 3:11-12).

   9.   **Seasons of *Solitude*.** "Greatly desiring to see thee, being mindful of thy tears, that I may be filled with joy," (2 Timothy 1:4).

   10.   **Seasons of *Suffering*.** "If we suffer, we shall also reign with Him: if we deny Him, He also will deny us," (2 Timothy 2:12).

   11.   **Seasons of *Warfare*.**   "Thou therefore endure hardness, as a good soldier of Jesus Christ. No man that warreth entangleth himself with the affairs of this life; that he may please Him Who hath chosen him to be a soldier," (2 Timothy 2:3-4).

   As I review the first half century of my life, I can distinguish the seasons.   In each season, I felt ignorant and unaware of the *purpose* of that specific season. I wondered, "How could God get any glory out of this situation?" Today, I see His Divine Design.

Did you ever see "The Karate Kid?" It contains some powerful lessons. In the story, the young boy desperately wanted to learn the art of fighting. His old mentor waited, and instead handed him a paint brush and instructed him to paint the fence. The young man was disheartened, but he followed the instructions of his mentor.

Discouraged, disillusioned and very disappointed, he could not see any relationship between painting the fence and fighting in the ring. When he finished, he was instructed to wash, wax and polish the car. As he moved his hands in a circular motion over the car, he was very demoralized. His thoughts were, "How will this help me in my future? How will this help me achieve my desire to be a great fighter?"

But the old mentor was secretly preparing each motion of his hands to *develop the movements of a fighter.* The young man did not discern it until much later.

Your Heavenly Father Knows What He Is Doing With Your Life. "But He knoweth the way that I take: when He hath tried me, I shall come forth as gold," (Job 23:10).

Some Seasons You May Not Understand His Workings. "Behold, I go forward, but He is not there; and backward, but I cannot perceive Him: On the left hand, where He doth work, but I cannot behold Him: He hideth Himself on the right hand, that I cannot see Him," (Job 23:8-9).

Embrace The Present Season God Has Scheduled In Your Life. Extract every possible benefit. "Wherefore lift up the hands which hang down, and the feeble knees," (Hebrews 12:12).

You Will Survive The Fires of The Furnace. "Though I walk in the midst of trouble, Thou wilt revive me: Thou shalt stretch forth Thine hand against the wrath of mine enemies, and Thy right hand shall save me," (Psalm 138:7).

Seasons Perfect You For Your Assignment. "The Lord will perfect that which concerneth me," (Psalm 138:8).

Success Is Inevitable For The Prepared.

Remember: *Your Assignment Will Require Seasons of Preparation.*

You Will Only
    Be Remembered
For Your Obsession.

-MIKE MURDOCK

YOU WILL ONLY SUCCEED WHEN YOUR ASSIGNMENT BECOMES AN OBSESSION

Focus Is Magnetic.

When you focus your attention and time to achieving your Assignment, you will experience Favor.

Jesus Rebuked Those Who Broke His Focus. "But when He had turned about and looked on His disciples, He rebuked Peter, saying, Get thee behind Me, satan: for thou savourest not the things that be of God, but the things that be of men," (Mark 8:33).

The Apostle Paul Was Obsessed With His Assignment. It explains his remarkable victories over enemies, adversaries and even friends who misunderstood him. He explained his focus to the Philippians, "...this one thing I do, forgetting those things which are behind, and reaching forth unto those things which are before, I press toward the mark for the prize of the high calling of God in Christ Jesus," (Philippians 3:13-14).

He moved *away* from past hurts, failures and memories. Obviously, he had a *photograph* of those things God had placed before him.

6 Keys For Developing An Obsession For Your Assignment

1. Identify Any Distraction To Your Assignment. "...let us lay aside every weight, and the sin which doth so easily beset us, and let us run with patience the race that is set before us," (Hebrews 12:1).

2. Be Ruthless In Refusing Any Responsibilities Unrelated To Your Assignment. "No man that warreth entangleth himself with the affairs of this life; that he may please Him Who hath chosen him to be a soldier," (2 Timothy 2:4).

3. Become An Expert On Your Assignment. "Study to shew thyself approved unto God, a workman that needeth not to be ashamed, rightly dividing the word of truth," (2 Timothy 2:15).

4. Avoid Any Conversation With Those Who Disrespect Your Assignment. "But shun profane and vain babblings: for they will increase unto more ungodliness. But foolish and unlearned questions avoid, knowing that they do gender strifes," (2 Timothy 2:16, 23).

5. Prepare For Uncommon Adversity. Satan dreads the *completion* of your Assignment. Each act of obedience can destroy a thousand satanic plans and desires.

6. Disconnect From Any Relationship That Does Not Celebrate Your Obsession. "And if any man obey not our word by this epistle, note that man, and have no company with him, that he may be ashamed," (2 Thessalonians 3:14).

I must share with you a personal experience because I am certain it will happen to you in your future (if it has not already happened). My secretary handed me the telephone number of a friend I had known 25 years ago. He had not written me for 25 years. He had not telephoned me for 25 years. He had not sown a Seed in my ministry for 25 years. Suddenly, he telephoned several times. He came to my weekly Bible study. He sowed a generous Seed in my ministry. He wanted to have a meal together. I consented.

"Mike, I am making more than $20,000 a month. It is the most wonderful company I have ever been involved with. I want you to become a part of it with me."

"Well," I replied slowly, "I am very consumed with my ministry. I really do not have the time to develop a secondary income at this point in my life. But, I appreciate it."

He was stunned. "But I know that you will need a strong financial base when you retire in the future. It is easy. You know thousands of people. You do not have to do anything but ask me to come and present this multi-level marketing plan to your people. They will come because they know you personally. And, this product is the best on the market. People will always need this product. Your people *need* them."

Well, I was impressed with his $20,000 monthly income, but I had to be very direct with him. "I like your product. I believe everyone should have one. I will buy one from you. I will tell my friends about you, but I cannot get involved in selling them, because this product cannot consume my attention, efforts and time. It would be impossible for me to develop an obsession with this product. You see, I know that *I can only succeed with something that consumes me.*

Besides that, I have not had an instruction from the Lord to pursue a business with this product."

My instructions had already arrived. *My inner peace was proof I was in the center of my Assignment.*

There will always be others with wonderful ideas who offer you options to your Assignment. Any hours you spend with them is a waste of their time and yours.

I have never heard from this man since.

You see, he had no interest in my Assignment whatsoever. He was only interested in my involvement *with his dream.* I was merely *a vehicle to generate finances* back into his own life.

My secretary handed me another telephone message recently. It was from a dear friend well known in ministry circles. He had built an incredible work for God, but due to extreme adversity had experienced some major losses in his personal life and in his ministry. I returned the telephone call.

"Mike, we have got to get together soon."

"Great! When do you want to meet?"

"Could you meet me tonight?" was his reply.

I could not imagine why this man wanted to meet with me so urgently. He had not telephoned me twice in the previous eight years. Suddenly, it was life and death. We met and talked. He was involved in a multi-level marketing program. He would succeed and I knew that. I also realized that anyone linked to him would have significant success. He is a remarkable, brilliant and enjoyable friend.

But he had a *different focus.*

I was very direct. "I really believe you could succeed significantly in this business. But, do you feel that this would distract you from the calling of God for ministry?"

"Oh, I will continue to have my ministry, but this will help people financially everywhere."

I replied, "My obsession is The Holy Spirit and spending time in The Secret Place. I have known more peace and joy since building my days around His presence than I have ever known in my lifetime. Wealth is wonderful. But doing the will of God and being in the center of my Assignment is my obsession," I replied carefully.

I have not heard from him again.

When You Make Your Assignment Your Obsession, Wrong Relationships Will Die. Right relationships will be born. The best way to disconnect from wrong people is to become obsessed with doing the right thing.

When Your Obsession Is To Do The Right Thing, Wrong People Will Find You Unbearable.

Fight For Your Focus.

Battle hard. Build walls that guarantee your concentration. Ignore the jeers, laughter and criticism that you are "obsessed."

Only The Obsessed Succeed.

Remember: *You Will Only Succeed When Your Assignment Becomes An Obsession.*

DECISION

Will You Accept Jesus As Your Personal Savior Today?

The Bible says, "That if thou shalt confess with thy mouth the Lord Jesus, and shalt believe in thine heart that God hath raised Him from the dead, thou shalt be saved," (Romans 10:9).

Pray this prayer from your heart today!

"Dear Jesus, I believe that You died for me and rose again on the third day. I confess I am a sinner...I need Your love and forgiveness...Come into my heart. Forgive my sins. I receive Your eternal life. Confirm Your love by giving me peace, joy and supernatural love for others. Amen."

DR. MIKE MURDOCK

is in tremendous demand as one of the most dynamic speakers in America today.

More than 16,000 audiences in 40 countries have attended his Schools of Wisdom and conferences. Hundreds of invitations come to him from churches, colleges and business corporations. He is a noted author of over 200 books, including the best sellers, *The Leadership Secrets of Jesus* and *Secrets of the Richest Man Who Ever Lived*. Thousands view his weekly television program, *Wisdom Keys with Mike Murdock*. Many attend his Schools of Wisdom that he hosts in many cities of America.

Clip and Mail

☐ Yes, Mike! I made a decision to accept Christ as my personal Savior today. Please send me my free gift of your book, *31 Keys to a New Beginning* to help me with my new life in Christ.

NAME _____ BIRTHDAY _____

ADDRESS _____

CITY _____ STATE ____ ZIP ____

PHONE _____ E-MAIL _____

Mail to: **The Wisdom Center** · 4051 Denton Hwy. · Ft. Worth, TX 76117
1-817-759-BOOK · 1-817-759-0300
You Will Love Our Website...! WisdomOnline.com

DR. MIKE MURDOCK

1 Has embraced his Assignment to Pursue...Proclaim...and Publish the Wisdom of God to help people achieve their dreams and goals.

2 Preached his first public sermon at the age of 8.

3 Preached his first evangelistic crusade at the age of 15.

4 Began full-time evangelism at the age of 19, which has continued since 1966.

5 Has traveled and spoken to more than 16,000 audiences in 40 countries, including East and West Africa, the Orient, Europe and South America.

6 Noted author of over 200 books, including best sellers, *Wisdom for Winning, Dream Seeds, The Double Diamond Principle, The Law of Recognition* and *The Holy Spirit Handbook.*

7 Created the popular *Topical Bible* series for Businessmen, Mothers, Fathers, Teenagers; *The One-Minute Pocket Bible* series, and *The Uncommon Life* series.

8 The Creator of The Master 7 Mentorship System, an Achievement Program for Believers.

9 Has composed thousands of songs such as "I Am Blessed," "You Can Make It," "God Rides On Wings Of Love" and "Jesus, Just The Mention Of Your Name," recorded by many gospel artists.

10 Is the Founder and Senior Pastor of The Wisdom Center, in Fort Worth, Texas...a Church with International Ministry around the world.

11 Host of *Wisdom Keys with Mike Murdock,* a weekly TV Program seen internationally.

12 Has appeared often on TBN, CBN, BET, Daystar, Inspirational Network, LeSea Broadcasting and other television network programs.

13 Has led over 3,000 to accept the call into full-time ministry.

THE MINISTRY

1 **Wisdom Books & Literature** - Over 200 best-selling Wisdom Books and 70 Teaching Tape Series.

2 **Church Crusades** - Multitudes are ministered to in crusades and seminars throughout America in "The Uncommon Wisdom Conferences." Known as a man who loves pastors, he has focused on church crusades for over 42 years.

3 **Music Ministry** - Millions have been blessed by the anointed songwriting and singing of Mike Murdock, who has made over 15 music albums and CDs available.

4 **Television** - *Wisdom Keys with Mike Murdock,* a nationally-syndicated weekly television program.

5 **The Wisdom Center** - The Church and Ministry Offices where Dr. Murdock speaks weekly on Wisdom for The Uncommon Life.

6 **Schools of The Holy Spirit** - Mike Murdock hosts Schools of The Holy Spirit in many churches to mentor believers on the Person and Companionship of The Holy Spirit.

7 **Schools of Wisdom** - In many major cities Mike Murdock hosts Schools of Wisdom for those who want personalized and advanced training for achieving "The Uncommon Dream."

8 **Missions Outreach** - Dr. Mike Murdock's overseas outreaches to 40 countries have included crusades in East and West Africa, the Orient, Europe and South America.

JOIN THE
Wisdom Key 3000
TODAY!

Will You Become My Ministry Partner In The Work of God?

Dear Friend,

God has connected us!

I have asked The Holy Spirit for 3000 Special Partners who will plant a monthly Seed of $58.00 to help me bring the gospel around the world. (58 represents 58 kinds of blessings in the Bible.)

Will you become my monthly Faith Partner in The Wisdom Key 3000? Your monthly Seed of $58.00 is so powerful in helping heal broken lives. When you sow into the work of God, 4 Miracle Harvests are guaranteed in Scripture, Isaiah 58...

- ▸ Uncommon Health (Isaiah 58)
- ▸ Uncommon Wisdom For Decision-Making (Isaiah 58)
- ▸ Uncommon Financial Favor (Isaiah 58)
- ▸ Uncommon Family Restoration (Isaiah 58)

Your Faith Partner,

Mike Murdock

P.S. Please clip the coupon attached and return it to me today, so I can rush the Wisdom Key Partnership Pak to you...or call me at 1-817-759-0300.

☐ *Yes Mike, I want to join The Wisdom Key 3000.*
  Please rush The Wisdom Key Partnership Pak to me today!
☐ *Enclosed is my first monthly Seed-Faith Promise of:*
    ☐ *$58* ☐ *Other $_____.*

☐ CHECK   ☐ MONEY ORDER   ☐ AMEX   ☐ DISCOVER   ☐ MASTERCARD   ☐ VISA

Credit Card # _____ Exp. ____/____

Signature _____

Name _____ Birth Date ____/____/____

Address _____

City _____ State _____ Zip _____

Phone _____ E-Mail _____

WK304

THE WISDOM CENTER
4051 Denton Highway • Fort Worth, TX 76117   **1-817-759-0300**

You Will Love Our Website:
WisdomOnline.com

It Could Happen To You!

Changes In Alzheimer's Disease...!

When you were at our church in Baltimore, in March of this year, I planted a $58 Seed for my mother's health and well-being. She will be 97 years old on May 27th and the doctor said Alzheimer's. We did not accept that diagnosis. About three weeks ago, we began to see and hear such a dramatic change in my mother that I know, and my family agrees, that God moved on her behalf. We expect her to have many more fruitful years.   B. - MD

Salvation of Husband...!

I sowed $5.80 three weeks ago, I received a $249 check, now I am sowing $58 x 2 ≈ $116 in my church, and I gave a command to my Seed for the 1,000 times more.

Today my husband received the Lord in my church in Vega Baja, this is one of the miracles I was looking for in 58 days.   N. - P.R.

New Job After 3 Months Of Unemployment...!

I sent $58 awhile back for my husband who had not worked in 3 months. He now has a good job!   D. - TX

$14,000 Miracle...!

I had sent in a check for $58 on the 58 Covenant of Blessings. That day we received a check for $5,000 in the mail and a promise from my in-laws to pay off the rest of our land...mortgage at the bank for over $14,000. Praise the Lord!   C. - IN

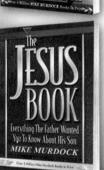

Crisis 7 BOOK PAK!

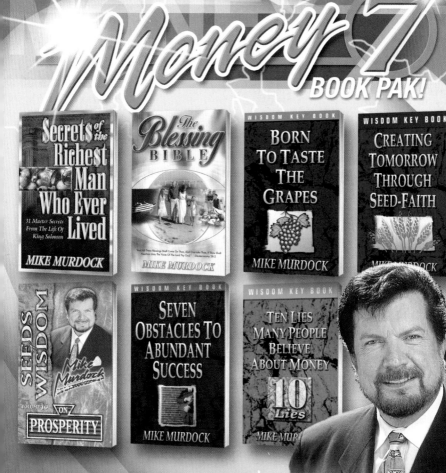

Money 7 BOOK PAK!

DR. MIKE MURDOCK

❶ **Secrets of the Richest Man Who Ever Lived** (Book/B-99/179pg/$12)

❷ **The Blessing Bible** (Book/B-28/252pg/$10)

❸ **Born To Taste The Grapes** (Book/B-65/32pg/$3)

❹ **Creating Tomorrow Through Seed-Faith** (Book/B-06/32pg/$5)

❺ **Seeds of Wisdom on Prosperity** (Book/B-22/32pg/$5)

❻ **Seven Obstacles To Abundant Success** (Book/B-64/32pg/$5)

❼ **Ten Lies Many People Believe About Money** (Book/B-04/32pg/$5)

Each Wisdom Book may be purchased separately if so desired.

The Wisdom Center
Money 7 Book Pak!
Only $**30** $45 Value
WBL-30
Wisdom Is The Principal Thing

Add 20% For S/H

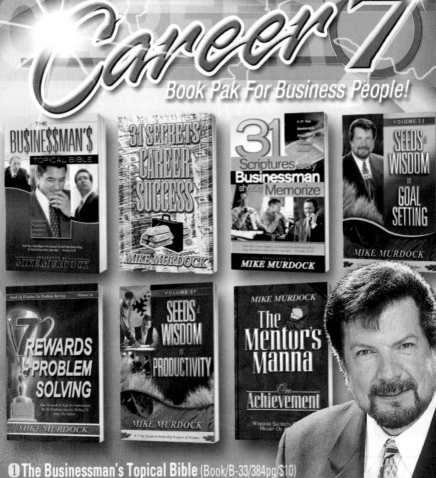

Career 7
Book Pak For Business People!

DR. MIKE MURDOCK

❶ **The Businessman's Topical Bible** (Book/B-33/384pg/$10)

❷ **31 Secrets for Career Success** (Book/B-44/114pg/$10)

❸ **31 Scriptures Every Businessman Should Memorize** (Book/B-141/32pg/$3)

❹ **Seeds of Wisdom on Goal-Setting** (Book/B-127/32pg/$5)

❺ **7 Rewards of Problem Solving** (Book/B-118/32pg/$7)

❻ **Seeds of Wisdom on Productivity** (Book/B-137/32pg/$5)

❼ **The Mentor's Manna on Achievement** (Book/B-79/32pg/$3)

Each Wisdom Book may be purchased separately if so desired.

The Wisdom Center
Career 7 Book Pak!
Only $**30** $43 Value
WBL-27
Wisdom Is The Principal Thing

Add 20% For S/H

D THE WISDOM CENTER
4051 Denton Highway • Fort Worth, TX 76117
1-817-759-BOOK
1-817-759-0300

You Will Love Our Website...!
WISDOMONLINE.COM

101 Wisdom Keys That Have Most Changed My Life.

SERIES 2
The
SCHOOL
of
WISDOM

101 WISDOM KEYS THAT HAVE MOST CHANGED MY LIFE

MIKE MURDOCK

THE LAWS OF LIFE SERIES

The
Law of
Recognition

Discovering the Gifts, Opportunities, & Relationships That God Has Already Placed In Your Life

999.9 FINE

MIKE MURDOCK

TS-42

101 WISDOM KEYS THAT HAVE MOST CHANGED MY LIFE
DR. MIKE MURDOCK

School of Wisdom #2 Pak!

- ▶ What Attracts Others Toward You
- ▶ The Secret Of Multiplying Your Financial Blessings
- ▶ What Stops The Flow Of Your Faith
- ▶ Why Some Fail And Others Succeed
- ▶ How To Discern Your Life Assignment
- ▶ How To Create Currents Of Favor With Others
- ▶ How To Defeat Loneliness
- ▶ 47 Keys In Recognizing The Mate God Has Approved For You
- ▶ 14 Facts You Should Know About Your Gifts And Talents
- ▶ 17 Important Facts You Should Remember About Your Weakness
- ▶ And Much, Much More...

The Wisdom Center
School of Wisdom #2 Pak!
Only $**30** $40 Value
PAK002
Wisdom Is The Principal Thing

Add 20% For S/H

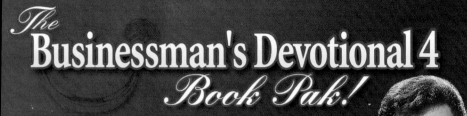
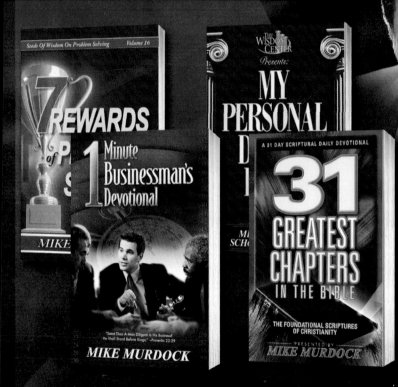

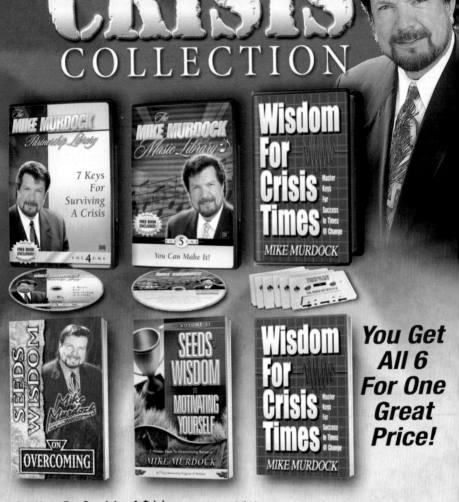

THE TURNAROUND Collection

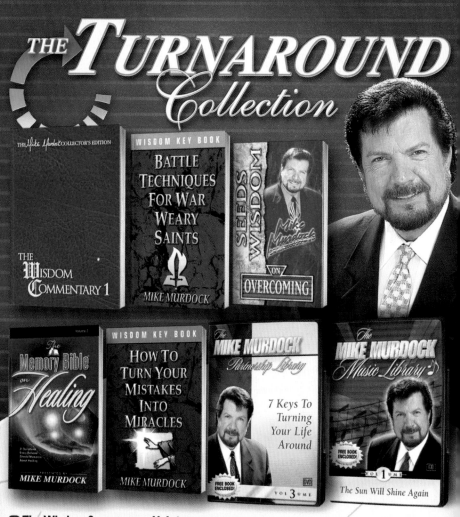

1. **The Wisdom Commentary Vol. 1** (Book/B-136/256pg/52 Topics/$25)

2. **Battle Techniques For War-Weary Saints** (Book/B-07/32pg/$5)

3. **Seeds of Wisdom on Overcoming** (Book/B-17/32pg/$3)

4. **The Memory Bible on Healing** (Book/B-196/32pg/$5)

5. **How To Turn Your Mistakes Into Miracles** (Book/B-56/32pg/$5)

6. **7 Keys To Turning Your Life Around** (DVD/MMPL-03D/$10)

7. **The Sun Will Shine Again** (Music CD/MMML-01/$10)

The Wisdom Center
The Turnaround Collection
Only **$40** $63 Value
PAK-15
Wisdom Is The Principal Thing

Add 20% For S/H

Each Wisdom Product may be purchased separately if so desired.

Financial $ecrets.

THE WISDOM BIBLE
Partnership Edition

Over 120 Wisdom Study Guides Included Such As:

- ▶ 10 Qualities Of Uncommon Achievers
- ▶ 18 Facts You Should Know About The Anointing
- ▶ 21 Facts To Help You Identify Those Assigned To You
- ▶ 31 Facts You Should Know About Your Assignment
- ▶ 8 Keys That Unlock Victory In Every Attack
- ▶ 22 Defense Techniques To Remember During Seasons Of Personal Attack
- ▶ 20 Wisdom Keys And Techniques To Remember During An Uncommon Battle
- ▶ 11 Benefits You Can Expect From God
- ▶ 31 Facts You Should Know About Favor
- ▶ The Covenant Of 58 Blessings
- ▶ 7 Keys To Receiving Your Miracle
- ▶ 16 Facts You Should Remember About Contentious People
- ▶ 5 Facts Solomon Taught About Contracts
- ▶ 7 Facts You Should Know About Conflict
- ▶ 6 Steps That Can Unlock Your Self-Confidence
- ▶ And Much More!

Your Partnership makes such a difference in The Wisdom Center Outreach Ministries. I wanted to place a Gift in your hand that could last a lifetime for you and your family...**The Wisdom Study Bible.**

40 Years of Personal Notes...this Partnership Edition Bible contains 160 pages of my Personal Study Notes...that could forever change your Bible Study of The Word of God. This **Partnership Edition...**is my personal **Gift of Appreciation** when you sow your Sponsorship Seed of $1,000 to help us complete The Prayer Center and TV Studio Complex. An Uncommon Seed Always Creates An Uncommon Harvest!

Mike

Thank you from my heart for your Seed of Obedience (Luke 6:38).

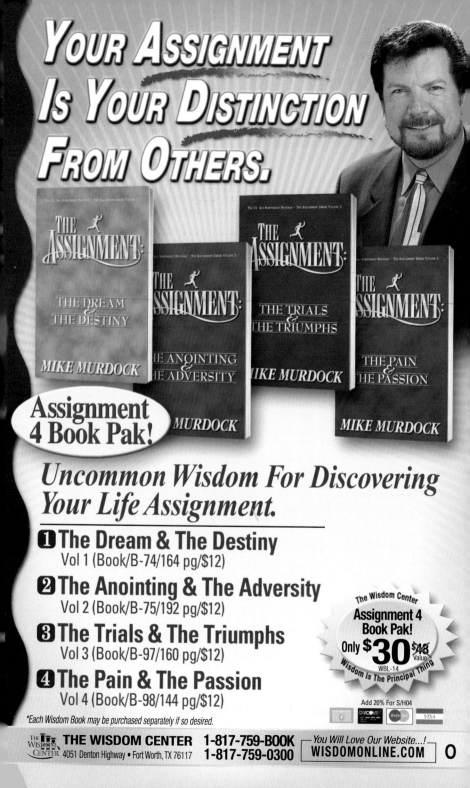

JOIN THE
Wisdom Key 3000
TODAY!

Thank You For Joining
The Wisdom Key 3000!

Will You Become My Ministry Partner In The Work Of God?

Dear Friend,

God has connected us!

I have asked The Holy Spirit for 3000 Special Partners who will plant a monthly Seed of $58.00 to help me bring the gospel around the world. (58 represents 58 kinds of blessings in the Bible.)

Will you become my monthly Faith Partner in The Wisdom Key 3000? Your monthly Seed of $58.00 is so powerful in helping heal broken lives. When you sow into the work of God, 4 Miracle Harvests are guaranteed in Scripture, Isaiah 58...

- ▶ Uncommon <u>Health</u> (Isaiah 58)
- ▶ Uncommon <u>Wisdom</u> For <u>Decision-Making</u> (Isaiah 58)
- ▶ Uncommon <u>Financial Favor</u> (Isaiah 58)
- ▶ Uncommon <u>Family Restoration</u> (Isaiah 58)

Your Faith Partner,

Mike Murdock

P.S. Please clip the coupon attached and return it to me today, so I can rush the Wisdom Key Partnership Pak to you...or call me at 1-817-759-0300.

THE **Covenant** OF Fifty-Eight **Blessings**
MIKE MURDOCK

101 **WISDOM KEYS**

The **Blessing** BIBLE
MIKE MURDOCK

WISDOM KEY 3000 PARTNERSHIP SEED BOOK

PP-03

☐ *Yes Mike, I want to join The Wisdom Key 3000.*
  Please rush The Wisdom Key Partnership Pak to me today!

☐ *Enclosed is my first monthly Seed-Faith Promise of:*
    ☐ **$58** ☐ **Other $_____.**

☐ CHECK ☐ MONEY ORDER ☐ AMEX ☐ DISCOVER ☐ MASTERCARD ☐ VISA

Credit Card # _____ Exp. _____/_____

Signature _____

Name _____ Birth Date _____/_____

Address _____

City _____ State _____ Zip _____

Phone _____ E-Mail _____

Your Seed-Faith Offerings are used to support The Wisdom Center, and all of its programs. The Wisdom Center reserves the right to redirect funds as needed in order to carry out our charitable purpose. In the event The Wisdom Center receives more funds for the project than needed, the excess will be used for another worthy outreach. (Your transactions may be electronically deposited.)

WK-304

P THE WISDOM CENTER **1-817-759-BOOK**
   4051 Denton Highway • Fort Worth, TX 76117 **1-817-759-0300**

You Will Love Our Website...!
WISDOMONLINE.COM